W9-AHY-748

ENDANGERED!

CROCODILES & ALLIGATORS

John Woodward

Series Consultant: James G. Doherty
General Curator, The Bronx Zoo, New York

BENCHMARK BOOKS

MARSHALL CAVENDISH

NEW YORK

7812704

Benchmark Books
Marshall Cavendish Corporation
99 White Plains Road
Tarrytown, New York 10591-9001

© Marshall Cavendish Corporation, 1999

All rights reserved. No part of this book may be reproduced or utilized in any form or by any means electronic or mechanical including photocopying, recording, or by any information storage and retrieval system, without permission from the copyright holders.

Library of Congress Cataloging-in-Publication Data

Woodward, John, 1954–
    Crocodiles & alligators / John Woodward.
        p. cm. — (Endangered!)
    Includes bibliographic references and index.
    Summary: Examines the physical characteristics, behavior, and life
cycle of crocodiles and alligators, describes the different kinds,
and discusses their endangered status.
    ISBN 0-7614-0322-1 (lib. bdg.)
    1. Crocodiles—Juvenile literature. 2. Alligators—Juvenile
literature. 3. Endangered species—Juvenile literature.
[1. Crocodiles. 2. Alligators. 3. Endangered species.] I. Title.
II. Series.
QL666.C925W66 1999
597.98—dc21   98-3894
                                                                  CIP
                                                                   AC

Printed in Hong Kong

PICTURE CREDITS
The publishers would like to thank the Natural History Photographic Agency (NHPA) for supplying all the photographs used in this book except for the following: 6, 12, 16, 17, 19, 21, 23, 26, 28, 29 Corbis UK Ltd.

Series created by Brown Packaging

Front cover: Nile crocodile.
Title page: Philippines crocodile.
Back cover: Nile crocodiles basking.

Contents

Introduction

Crocodiles are awesome creatures. They look like nothing else on Earth. With their scaly, armored skin, terrifying jaws, razor-sharp teeth, and cold stare they look and behave like prehistoric monsters. And so they should, because that is exactly what they are.

Crocodiles are survivors from prehistoric times. They first appeared about 200 million years ago, at about the same time as the dinosaurs. For about 135 million years crocodiles lived in swamps and rivers while dinosaurs ruled the land. Some of these early crocodiles were big enough to attack and kill massive plant-eating dinosaurs in just the same way as modern Nile crocodiles kill zebras.

Crocodiles are strange-looking creatures with a scaly skin, short legs, and a long, powerful tail.

4

The dinosaurs disappeared about 65 million years ago, but the crocodiles lived on. Nobody knows why. Many scientists believe that the dinosaurs were wiped out when a giant **asteroid** crashed into Earth, so maybe the crocodiles had some special feature that, by pure luck, helped them survive. If so, then they still have it, because they have not changed much over the last 65 million years. They were perfectly **adapted** for their way of life then, and they have had little reason to change much since.

Crocodiles are **reptiles**. They are **relatives** of lizards, snakes, and tortoises. Reptiles share many of the same features. These include a tough, waterproof skin. The skin

Areas where crocodiles and their close relatives can be found

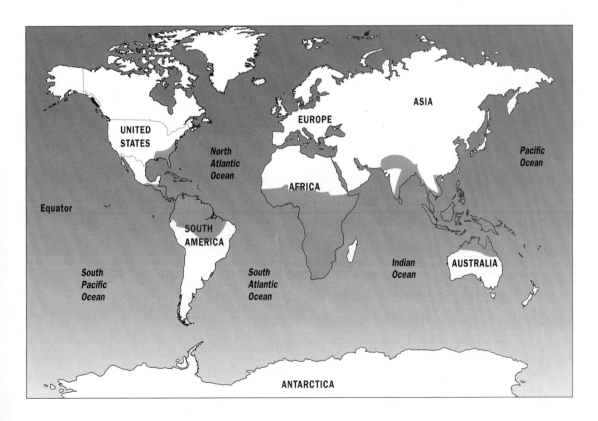

Crocodiles have a tough waterproof skin. There are bony plates under the scales to make the skin harder.

has thick, horny scales to make it stronger. Crocodiles also have plates of bone in the skin. These form a bony armor beneath the scales of a crocodile's back.

Like all reptiles, crocodiles are "cold-blooded." This is an odd thing to call them, because most of the time their blood is as warm as ours. The difference is that, unlike warm-blooded animals, crocodiles cannot keep warm by turning food energy into heat. They have to warm up by basking in the sun or by lying in warm water. Since their bodies must be reasonably warm to work properly, crocodiles live in places where the **climate** is hot enough to keep them at the right temperature. This is why most crocodiles live in places like Africa and India.

As long as a crocodile stays warm enough, being cold-blooded is actually useful. Warm-blooded animals use a lot of energy just running their central heating systems, so they have to eat a lot. A tiger that weighs the same as a crocodile has to eat 20 times as much, just to keep warm. This means catching 20 times as many animals, which is hard work. It also means that every tiger needs a lot of space to live in, so it can find enough animals to eat. Crocodiles do not have this problem. At least 20 tiger-sized crocodiles can live in the space needed by one tiger. They can also go without food for a long time without getting sick.

All crocodiles are good at hunting in the water. They sometimes leap out of the water to grab animals who come too close to the water's edge. Although crocodiles have short legs, they can still move quite fast on land.

Crocodiles spend most of the day basking in the sun. They open their mouths so that the heat of the sun can help warm their blood.

This crocodile is waiting to catch its dinner. Crocodiles can float in the water for hours with just their eyes and their nostrils showing.

In the water, crocodiles are deadly. Driven by its long tail, a crocodile can swim amazingly fast. By simply breathing out it can sink without a trace and stay hidden underwater like a submarine. It can lie in ambush with just its eyes and nostrils above the surface. A special flap in its throat closes its windpipe. This enables the animal to open its mouth underwater and seize **prey** without drowning.

Seizing prey is what crocodiles are all about. Most have 60 to 80 stout, pointed teeth that sprout in ragged rows from their long, powerful jaws. The rows look ragged because each tooth is replaced by a new one as it wears out, so some teeth are older and longer than others.

Crocodiles continue growing new teeth throughout their lives. They never have the problem of losing their teeth as they get older. With all their teeth in order, they can keep eating and stay healthy. Crocodiles can live to be very old. Some have lived to be 100 or more!

Surprisingly, considering all those teeth, crocodiles cannot chew. Most can bite with terrific force, crushing the shells of turtles as if they were eggshells, but they cannot bite pieces off large prey. Sometimes a crocodile catches something that is too big to swallow whole. It deals with the problem by grabbing part of the body in its jaws and spinning around in the water to rip it off. Sometimes other crocodiles join in so that they can get something to eat, too. Crocodiles often work together to tear their prey apart. They are a lot smarter than they look.

All crocodiles lay eggs. The eggs look rather like hens' eggs, with softer shells, and the mother crocodile lays them in a pit or a mound of leaves and grass. She watches over

Crocodiles lay their eggs in mounds of earth or leaves. The females build the nests and guard the eggs from enemies.

the nest until the eggs hatch. When the baby crocodiles appear, the mother digs them out and helps them to the water. She often carries them in her mouth, holding them carefully so they are not harmed by her fearsome teeth.

The babies are perfect tiny copies of their parents. They can hunt for themselves right away, starting on insects and small fish and moving onto bigger prey as they grow.

Baby crocodiles have their problems, though. Many are eaten, sometimes by other crocodiles. Only about two in every hundred babies survive to become adults and produce young of their own. If more are killed by humans, then the crocodile population gradually dwindles to nothing. And they *are* killed, in large numbers, for their valuable skin. Tanned and polished, the skin is turned into shoes, purses,

A female crocodile with her baby. The young crocodile has just hatched. The mother is carrying it to the water.

Sadly, many crocodiles and alligators are hunted for their skin. It is used to make shoes, handbags, and belts.

belts, briefcases, and wallets. Some crocodiles are actually kept in special farms for their skin, but most of the things made of crocodile skin that you see in stores are made from the hides of wild animals. Conservationists think that some three million Nile crocodiles were killed for their skins between 1950 and 1980. Not surprisingly these amazing creatures are dying out.

Crocodiles are also running out of living space. Swamps are drained to make fertile farmland, and riverbanks are built over. People are scared of crocodiles and don't want to live near them. So most crocodiles are now much rarer than they once were. Some are in danger of disappearing all together. Since they are our last link with the dinosaurs, that would be a real shame.

Typical Crocodiles

The biggest, most dangerous crocodiles belong to a group sometimes called the "typical crocodiles" to distinguish them from alligators and the strange-looking gharial.

The easiest way to tell the difference between a crocodile and an alligator is to look at their teeth. When a crocodile closes its mouth, you can still see the fourth tooth from the front on the bottom jaw. The upper jaw has a special notch in it to make room. An alligator does not have this notch, so its smile is not so crooked.

You would normally avoid getting close enough to look at the teeth, because some of these "typical crocodiles" eat people. The Nile crocodile of central and southern Africa

A crocodile's smile. You can tell a crocodile from an alligator by looking at its jaws. Crocodiles show their teeth even with their jaws shut.

has been known to attack people. But the most dangerous killer of all is the Indopacific or saltwater crocodile, which lives on the tropical shores of the Indian and Pacific Oceans. Most crocodiles can only live in fresh water, but this is one of the few that can swim out to sea. It lives in river **estuaries** as well as inland rivers and marshes. It has a huge **range**, from India and Southeast Asia to northern Australia. It often causes trouble everywhere it goes.

An Indopacific crocodile can grow up to 23 feet (7 m) long and weigh up to three tons (3,050 kg), making it the biggest living reptile. It has an appetite to match, eating virtually any animal it can catch – including people. Most of the people

Area where Nile crocodiles can be found

AFRICA

Indian Ocean

Atlantic Ocean

Crocodiles have short legs but can still move quite fast on land.

13

Typical Crocodiles

killed by crocodiles from India to Australia have fallen victim to this **species**. As a result the Indopacific crocodile is considered to be a pest. Its skin is very valuable, because it is large and contains fewer bony plates than the skins of other species. As a result vast numbers are shot each year, and it is becoming rare almost everywhere it lives.

Over on the other side of the Pacific, the American crocodile has a similar way of life. Like the Indopacific crocodile it is happy to live in salt water, and this has allowed it to spread to most of the larger Caribbean islands such as Jamaica, Cuba, and Hispaniola. It also lives on the southern tip of Florida, and all along the Central American coast from Mexico to Venezuela, and to Peru on the Pacific side. The American crocodile is smaller than its Indopacific cousin,

Areas where Indopacific crocodiles can be found

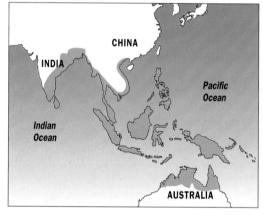

Underwater picture of an Indopacific crocodile. These crocodiles are at home in saltwater and fresh water.

growing to about 16 feet (5 m) long. The American crocodile is also quite timid, so it is far less dangerous. It has relatively narrow jaws and feeds mainly on fish.

The American crocodile has disappeared from many places where it was once common. The main reason for this is hunting for its skin. People are building homes and roads in the coastal areas where the crocodiles live. This is another reason why the numbers are dropping. Although the American crocodile is protected by law throughout most of its range, it is declining almost everywhere except Florida. In Jamaica, for example, a population of about 2,000 in 1969 plummeted to only 41 within 15 years.

The very similar Orinoco crocodile is even more rare. Much the same size as the American crocodile, it lives in the deep, wide stretches of the Orinoco river in northern South America. During the tropical rainy season it spreads out across the flooded forests and grasslands feeding on fish, small **mammals**, and birds. It comes back to the river

Crocodiles will eat almost any kind of prey. This crocodile has captured a frog that strayed too close to the reptile's snapping jaws.

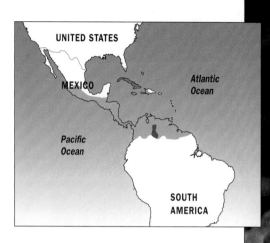

Areas where the American crocodile (green), the Orinoco crocodile (purple), and the Cuban crocodile (red) can be found

when the floods go down. The Orinoco crocodile's hide is worth a lot of money, and the animal has been hunted to the point of near-extinction. Luckily it is being bred in captivity, and many of these captive-bred crocodiles have been released in protected parts of the Orinoco river.

All over the world, the most vulnerable rare animals are those that live on islands, because they have nowhere else to go when their **habitat** is destroyed. Crocodiles are no exception, and two species, the Cuban crocodile and Philippines crocodile, are disappearing fast because their wild habitat is being destroyed.

Despite their sharp teeth, crocodiles cannot chew. They tear off chunks of meat and swallow them whole.

The Cuban crocodile is small, growing to about 11 feet (3.5 m) at most. Its short, broad snout gives it the biting power to feed on turtles and other tough prey, which it finds in the wetlands of coastal Cuba. Unfortunately many of these areas are being drained to make farmland. Today the crocodile only lives in protected parts of swampland in southwest Cuba. It has suffered from **crossbreeding** with the American crocodile. Many so-called Cuban crocodiles are actually **hybrids** or mixtures of the two species.

The even smaller Philippines crocodile is one of the rarest crocodiles of all, for there are only about 100 animals left. They are scattered over the marshes and lakes of four Philippine islands. These are Mindoro, Negros, Mindanao, and Samar. The crocodiles live in such small groups that they seem almost bound to die out in the wild. Most of the

An Orinoco crocodile rests in grassland in Venezuela. The skin of this species is particularly prized by hunters.

habitat suitable for crocodiles has been turned into farmland. Much of the land has been contaminated by **pollution** from copper mines.

Both the Cuban crocodile and Philippines crocodile are being bred in captivity. Sadly they can only be released into small wildlife sanctuaries. It seems there is little chance of reviving the wild **populations**.

Areas where Siamese crocodiles (green) and Philippines crocodiles (red) can be found

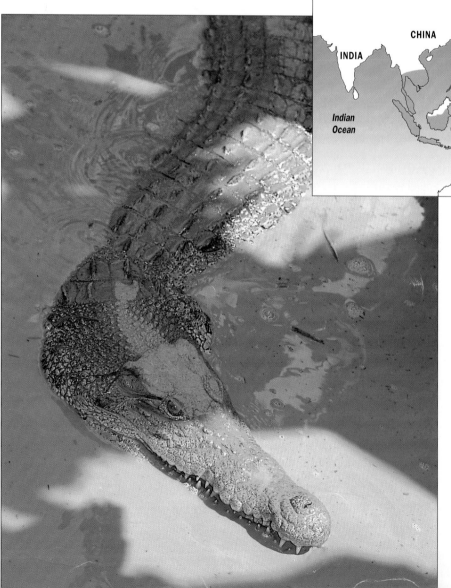

Philippines crocodiles like this one are threatened by destruction of the places where it lives.

Crocodile wrestlers grapple with the reptiles at the Samutprakarn crocodile farm in Thailand.

Across the South China Sea in Southeast Asia the Siamese crocodile is also endangered. This freshwater crocodile was once widespread from Vietnam and Thailand to Malaysia, but it has now vanished from most of the places where it used to live. Many creatures were shot for their hides and even for their meat. Throughout the region the remaining wildernesses are disappearing as forests are cut down and marshes drained to make space for paddy fields for growing rice.

Yet while the wild Siamese crocodile is virtually **extinct**, there are several thousand in captivity thanks to **captive breeding** on the Samutprakarn crocodile farm near Bangkok. If enough space is set aside for them in surviving areas of wilderness, these captive-bred crocodiles could be released into the wild. If the critically endangered Siamese crocodile can be saved like this, so can all the others.

Alligators and Caimans

An alligator is a crocodile with a difference, although the difference is very slight. Its skull has a few odd features, and all the teeth in its lower jaw are hidden when it closes its mouth. The caimans of South America are much the same, so alligators and caimans are probably descended from the same ancestors. Scientists group alligators and caimans together in the same family.

There are only two species of alligators, and they live in completely different parts of the world. The best-known is the American alligator of the southern United States. There is also a Chinese alligator, which lives in the River Yangtze. Compared to other crocodiles they both have an unusual

Two alligators resting on a river bank. Alligators have shorter snouts than crocodiles do.

ability to cope with cold weather, so they can live farther north. Alligators can even survive in regions where winter temperatures often fall well below freezing point. They cannot keep active at such times, but they can survive by staying in deep water, which is warmer than the icy shallows. If a layer of ice forms at the surface of an alligator's pool, the animal holds its nostrils above water to keep a small breathing hole open. Alligators have been found frozen into the ice like this, but still alive and well.

The American alligator normally grows to about 13 feet (4 m), although adults can reach 20 feet (6 m) if they live long enough.

Area where American alligators can be found

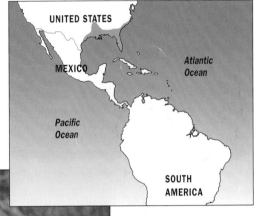

An American alligator warming itself in the sun. If the animal gets too hot, it will slide into the river to cool down.

The Chinese alligator is smaller than the American type. Its skin is less valuable too.

CHINA

INDIA

Pacific Ocean

Indian Ocean

It has a massive, flattened head with broad, powerful jaws. These are ideal for crushing the turtles, waterbirds, and small mammals that the alligator eats.

Area where Chinese alligators can be found

Big alligators sometimes catch farm animals such as calves and pigs as well as pet dogs. They are quite capable of attacking people, especially children. This has made the American alligator an unwelcome neighbor throughout its range. Huge numbers were shot in the past. By the 1950s, the combined effects of hunting, swamp drainage, and coastal housing and leisure parks made it so rare that it was declared an endangered, protected species.

Since then the American alligator has staged a comeback. In the 1950s, a **conservation** program banned hunting and in time allowed it to be removed from the endangered list. By the 1980s there were so many alligators in some parts of Florida that the wildlife authorities felt the need for an annual cull called the "Nuisance Alligator Control Program." The population of American alligators is growing and the animals have even become a tourist attraction!

Sadly the same cannot be said of the Chinese alligator. This timid animal is much smaller than its American cousin. It rarely grows to more than 6 feet (1.8 m) long.

Feeding time at an alligator park near Kissimmee, Florida where the American alligator is now a tourist attraction.

A spectacled caiman. A ridge across the animal's nose makes it look like it is wearing spectacles.

Area where spectacled caimans can be found

It was once widespread throughout eastern China in the rivers and lakes around the Yangtze, but it is now restricted to a relatively small region of **seasonal** marshland to the west of Shanghai. It feeds on turtles, fish, birds, and small mammals such as rats.

Naturally it has never been popular with the local people, who see it as a threat to fish and wild ducks as well as domestic animals, so large numbers of this alligator have been hunted. Most of its original habitat has been destroyed by **intensive farming** and by building.

In the 1980s, the Chinese government tried to save the alligator by starting a captive breeding program. The project has been very successful. Zoos in China and outside China worked together to save this species through captive breeding. Today there are only about 300 wild Chinese alligators left, but there are at least 1,000 in captivity.

Caimans live in the tropical rainforests of South and Central America. The most common is the spectacled caiman. This species has a huge range from southern Mexico to Paraguay. Vast numbers are shot for their skins but the spectacled caiman still survives thanks to its wide distribution. It is an **adaptable** creature, found in savanna lakes and rivers as well as swampy forests, and normally grows to about 8 feet (2.5 m) long.

The bigger black caiman can grow to 20 feet (6 m). It too has a wide range across most of the Amazon Basin. But its hide is much more valuable than that of the spectacled caiman. As a result it has been hunted more than its cousin. Local people hate caimans because they kill so many cattle. There is a caiman hunt in the Amazon each year. About 99 percent of the original population has been destroyed, and it is now extinct in many places where it was once common.

Area where black caimains live

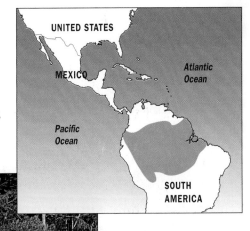

These men are taking a black caiman to a protected area where it can live safely away from hunters.

The Gharial

Crocodiles that feed mainly on fish have long, slender jaws armed with a lot of sharp, spiky teeth for trapping and gripping their slippery, struggling prey. There are several of these fish-catching species, including the African slender-snouted crocodile and the Australian freshwater crocodile, but the real expert at the job is the Indian gharial.

The gharial is a weird-looking animal. It is so different from crocodiles and alligators that it is put in its own special family. The gharial grows to some 23 feet (7 m) long. It is slimmer than most crocodiles and has very weak legs. Because of this it cannot walk well, so it usually stays

Gharials have a long snout with a bump at the end. The bump gives the animal its name, which comes from an Indian word for "pot."

close to the water. But its strangest feature is its long, narrow snout, which sticks out of its head like the beak of a bird. Unlike a bird, though, the gharial has teeth: about 100 of them. When it shuts its jaws the teeth lock together like a zipper. This makes a very effective fish trap.

The gharial cannot swim particularly fast, so it usually feeds by lying still in the water, waiting for an unwary fish to swim past. When the unlucky fish is close enough, the gharial sweeps its snout sideways to snap the fish up. Its narrow jaws make this easier because they move through the water more easily than the massive jaws of species like the Nile and Indopacific crocodiles. The gharial's jaws are too thin and weak to

Areas where gharials (green) and false gharials (red) can be found

CHINA

INDIA

Pacific Ocean

Indian Ocean

AUSTRALIA

This gharial has caught a fish. The gharial's sharp teeth are perfect for grasping its slippery prey.

capture large animals. So although these animals may look fearsome, they cannot harm people.

Gharials live in deep, fast-flowing rivers. Today there are two separate populations: one in Pakistan and western India in the region of the River Indus, and the other in eastern India, Nepal, and Bangladesh in the rivers Mahanadi, Ganges, and Brahmaputra. Gharials were once common from India to western China, but river-damming projects and hunting for their valuable hide has wiped them out in many areas. Until recently, they seemed likely to vanish.

In the early 1970s, there were fewer than 70 surviving adults. The Indian government began a conservation effort combined with a breeding program. Most wild gharials now live in big wildlife sanctuaries, where eggs are collected for

A gharial in the Royal Chitwan National Park in Nepal. The animal is protected in several parks in Nepal and India.

hatching in **incubators**, like chicks. The young gharials are reared in captivity until they are about 4 feet (1.2 m) long. When they are big enough to look after themselves, they are released. There are now over 2,000 animals in the wild, but until the number of animals in the wild increases the gharial will stay on the endangered list.

Farther south, in Sumatra, Malaysia, and Borneo, lives a crocodile known as the false gharial. Like the "real" gharial it has a slender snout adapted for fish catching, but it does not have the same beak-like look.

No one can agree what a false gharial is. Some scientists think it is one of the typical crocodiles. But other scientists say the animal is odd enough to be put in its own group.

The false gharial lives in swamps, lakes, and rivers. Its habitats are being destroyed to make way for farmland, and this has caused an alarming drop in the number of false gharials. Sadly the false gharial attracts little interest. While the gharial may revive, its southern look-alike may disappear before anyone notices.

The false gharial is one of the least known of all the crocodile relatives. This makes it hard for scientists to protect the species.

Useful Addresses

For more information about crocodiles and how you can help protect them, contact these organizations:

Crocodile Specialist Group
Florida Museum of Natural History
University of Florida
Gainesville, FL 32611

Division of Endangered Species
Washington Office
Branch of Information Management
US Fish and Wildlife Service
Mail Stop 452ARLSQ
1849 C St., NW
Washington, D.C. 20240

World Wildlife Fund
1250 24th Street NW
Washington, D.C. 20037

World Wildlife Fund Canada
90 Eglinton Avenue East
Suite 504
Toronto
Ontario M4P 2Z7

Further Reading

Alligators and Crocodiles Michael Bright (New York: Franklin Watts, 1990)

Crocodiles and Alligators Lionel Bender (New York: Gloucester Press, 1988)

Crocodiles and Alligators of the World David Alderton (New York: Facts on File, 1990)

Endangered Wildlife of the World (New York: Marshall Cavendish Corporation, 1994)

Glossary

Adaptable: Able to change behavior to suit different conditions.

Adapted: Altered over thousands of years to suit different conditions.

Asteroid: A huge meteorite hurtling through space.

Captive breeding: Encouraging captive crocodiles to lay eggs.

Climate: The typical weather conditions of a region.

Conservation (Kon-ser-**VAY**-shun)**:** Working to help wild animals and plants to survive.

Crossbreeding: When two animals of different species mate and produce young.

Estuary: The mouth of a river, where it meets the salty sea.

Extinct: No longer living anywhere in the world.

Habitat: The place where an animal lives. For example, a Cuban crocodile's habitat is swampland.

Hybrid: An animal with parents of two different species.

Incubator: A heated container designed for keeping eggs warm so they develop properly.

Intensive farming: Squeezing as much produce from the land as possible.

Mammal: Warm-blooded, usually furry animals that feed their new-born young on milk.

Pollution: Materials such as garbage and chemicals that damage the environment.

Population: A number of animals that live in the same area and are able to breed together.

Prey: An animal that is hunted and eaten by another animal.

Range: The area of the world where an animal is found.

Relative: An animal that has features in common with another kind of animal.

Reptile: An animal with a backbone and a scaly skin that lays eggs.

Seasonal: Something that alters with the seasons, like a marsh that dries out in summer.

Species: A type of animal. Animals of the same species look alike and can breed together.

Index